Rare Space

Rare Space

Leslie Anne Mcilroy

Word Press

Copyright © 2001 by Leslie Anne Mcilroy
All Rights Reserved
ISBN: 0-9708667-0-4
LCCN: 2001087823

Published by Word Press
P.O. Box 541106
Cincinnati, OH 45254-1106

Cover Art: Pen and Ink Drawing by Michel Tsouris,
   copyright © 2001
Author Photo: John Clines, copyright © 2001

Editor: Kevin Walzer
Business Manager: Lori Jareo
Typeset in Crillee and Cheltenham by WordTech
   Communications, Cincinnati, Ohio
Printed in the United States by Morris Publishing, 3212
   East Highway 30, Kearney, NE 68847, 800-650-7888

Visit Word Press on the Web: www.word-press.com

Acknowledgments

Grateful acknowledgment is made to the editors of the following publications in which these works or earlier versions of them originally appeared:

Another Chicago Magazine: "Goodbye Valentine"
Eclectic Literary Forum Poetry Prize: "October"
The Ledge: "Sins"
Main Street Rag: "House Sitting"
Mississippi Review: "Big Brain"
The MacGuffin National Poet Competition: "Behind the
   Irises"and "How to Change a Flat"
The Pittsburgh Post-Gazette: "Ten Years in The Cage" and
   "1965"
The Pittsburgh Quarterly: "Debts," "Siesta" and "Gravel"
The Pittsburgh Quarterly On-Line: "Walking on Eggshells"

Thanks to the editors of these anthologies who published versions of the following poems:

American Poetry: The Next Generation: "Goodbye Valen-
   tine," "Siesta" and "How to Change a Flat"
Emily Dickinson Award Anthology: "Love Isn't Enough"
Henry's Creature: Poems and Stories on the Automobile:
   "How to Change a Flat"

A great debt also goes to the editors of Slipstream Press, Bob Borgatti, Dan Sicoli and Livio Farallo, for their enthusiasm, dedication and tireless promotion of the chapbook *Gravel* (Slipstream Publications, 1997) by Leslie Anne Mcilroy, in which a number of the included poems were first printed.

Love to Jan Beatty for her intimate friendship and ruthless skill in refining and revising; to Sapphire for her unflinching support; to Michel Tsouris for drawing the rarest of covers; to Terrance Hayes, Sean Thomas Dougherty, Allison Joseph, Timothy Liu, Jim Daniels, Hilary Masters, Roger Bell, Rick Kearns, and Charles Clifton for their poetic verve and emotional scaffolding; to my dear friends Sue Clifton, Tami Greene, Amy Hartman, Karen Demmler, Byron Nash, Carol Shrefler, Calvin Rambler, Danny Ferraro, Vic Curti and Tammy Ryan, who bought me drinks, gave me lines and shared my manias; to The Kaiser Group who suffered my efforts; to my family—my mother, brother and sister—for their constant sustenance; to Sam Maxwell II for his singular and lasting love; to Danny Morrow for his relentless belief; and finally, to my sweet Galen Switzer for being the perfect final line.

For Sam Maxwell II, Danny Morrow, and Galen Switzer.
My father. My friend. My lover forever.

Contents

1.

You have to get to the point where you can open up the memories so you can get to the spaces you can live with.

—Carole Maso

Siesta

I do errands early
on a day this hot,
putting the groceries
away before noon,
cutting lemons
arranged on the plate
like a sun burst.
I wear my wide
brimmed hat, tip
it back with the first
shot of Cuervo.

In this wooden
chair I read thin
books, the flat boards
of the porch
scorched and dry,
the way I imagine
it is in Arizona
or New Mexico—
there, the heat is un-
beatable and young
men grow skin
like leather to protect,
squinting occasionally
at the horizon
between swallows
of beer.

Now it is two,
and three lemons
are left. The line
of sun cuts the tips

of my toes, makes
my eyes crackle
like two thin leaves.
Turning the page
(I have finished
a chapter),
I find a note
in the margin
about forgiving
and rise to brush
the salt from my lap.

October

Somewhere in central Florida
my father lies buried, and with him
a fair part of my changing heart
milling restless in the soil
of that hot state, its crab
grass and sand so unlike Pittsburgh—
leaves ripe with the will
to scatter and fall.

If I could, I would bring him home,
back to the chill morning
that hoisted him up telephone poles
as a Bell lineman, hovering in a harness
above the street, leaning against
the sky like a casual visitor. He knew
which wires to cut, where to find
a weak connection.

At night, beneath an old Plymouth
he would work, slim and angular
with scoured blue eyes, skin rugged
and worn as I stood still in the damp
garage air—the smell of oil, the backward
silence of the October night claiming
its place between my breath
and the concrete floor. Dressed

in pajamas and without prayers,
I held the caged lantern light
so he could see, his knuckles
chapped and scraped
as he forced a piece of metal
into place and waved me closer,

greased the base of the thing
that would make the car run.
Then lighting a cigarette and wiping
the grease from his hands,
he slipped the denim jacket over
my shoulders, shut out the light,
wandered off to a warmer place.

Ten Years in The Cage

Mostly I am good
with Jack, offering to get
him coffee or a coke,
to call a taxi or a friend.
But nights when the gin
takes a back seat in his mouth
and he waves his glass,
spitting "pussycat" in that tired
late-shift slur, I turn and wait
for him to leave; the tide
of regret rising like the sharp
corner of a table—his belch
as he stumbles on the way out.

And it's thick some days,
the way you only hear
the bass line on the jukebox,
the air draped with that flat
fryer-smoke smell. Billy
in his sixth year of six nights
a week behind the bar,
6 p.m. to 2 a.m.
The revolving door
of waitresses—all writers
or dead heads, lesbians
or psych majors—struggling
to pay rent, to get laid;
too bored to figure tax
on a 2-dollar hoagie, sharp
as tin at totaling tips:
they never get stiffed twice.

Me, I take it on both
sides of the bar, stragglers
and sophists knee to knee
on a plowed row of stools,
straddling an Iron and a shot
of Windsor. Friday nights I find
my place in line, drink
for free; bathroom graffiti
like "my karma ran over
your dogma," rescued
from tiled obscurity,
old lovers dropping by
with memories as soft
as their bellies, kisses weary
as the fading neon,
last call rising
like the moon
over Forbes Avenue.

Grandma Talks to God

"I wonder what my life
would have been like
if I had had more confidence,"
my grandmother said, as if
she had forgotten the meltdown
in 1949 when she bashed
the new stove with a baseball bat,
denting the cool white metal,
the GE Electro-oven all crazy
and misshapen, the sauce
red and splattered across
the linoleum floor, thin
as her cavernous heart.

And the shock, the lightning
rods taped to her temple that left
her raw, the skin on her hands
scaled back to reveal the pulse
of blood and bare knuckles
below the surface. The hours
locked in the bathroom—sobs
like muted trombones—moaning
softly behind the tremorous beat
of her children outside the door,
unsure whether mother would bake
a cake for Sunday's dinner.

And how God came that day
in the kitchen as she listened
to the radio, peeling apples
for a pie. He came right through
the paper skin of her collarbone,
and she put down the peeler

to pray for a one-way ticket
to Switzerland where she might teach
Italian and finger small chocolates
on Friday afternoons, where
she would eat the apple whole,
spare the sugar, chew the peel.

The Weather with You

In the booth at Dee's Cafe,
her side of the seat
so much warmer than his—
coats and gloves
pressing gently on her thigh,
pressing her close to the cool
joint of his shoulder—
she was casually distracted
by the length of his fingers,
weary with saying the smart
thing, wanting only to rest.
His bones like bridges,
held him apart, separating
the heart and the skin—
a hollow span
that would be crossed
only once.

Later that night
in the fading porch light,
she slipped unaware
from her wraps and layers,
offered him a necklace
of water and sun.
And he, imagining for a moment
something rare and unchecked,
stood where love had left him—
having waited this long,
content to wait longer.

Removing the Polish

My fingernails break all the time
now, split when I button a blouse
or pull a staple, just today unhinging
the ice cube tray, it became clear
that I need some help.

And the edges are ragged
and dangerous, more
than you know, scraping
my face as I wash. The blood ripe,
and the scab along my right
temple thickening.

A size 8 is still too small
to fit the strain of my swelling hips,
the zipper ripping another nail
to the quick, the tips
of my fingers swelling
like pink nubs.

And polish clogs the shelf—
red, black and Camaro green—
purchased long ago, before
my hands shook
and my stomach ached
at the thought of milk.
Back when vomiting
only meant I would feel bad
for a while. Eat less.

They're just fingernails
after all, and they're dead.
Who could expect
them to be strong?

The Lottery

Five cops, five of them,
converge to frisk the Black boy
at the checkout. He's fifteen,
maybe sixteen—corn-rowed hair
and baggy jeans—the look
on his face the same I wear
going through airport security
when my steel wing tips
set off the alarm,
like this is just the way things are.
Except he's not flying anywhere
and no one likes his thin-eyed shrug
when they tell him to step away
from the register,
spread his legs, his arms,
like a dark pigeon
in a public square.
And I wonder if he's caught,
if he knifed someone, stole a fifth,
if the sharp silky angle
of his cheek bones
might cut me, if he takes
what he wants.
Is he thinking about hate,
what he could do with a gun?

I've got my copy of *People*
as the manager points
and the cops with their pants
tucked in their boots, come up
short. He's hiding nothing.
No knife. No gun.
And it looks like he's paid

for what he's got: chips and pop.
And the girls—maybe his friends,
his sisters—just keep talking,
roll their eyes when the head cop
mutters a warning and onlookers
look away, search for Advantage
Cards, pay with a VISA.

And the cashier,
a Black woman
who never once looked up,
she's watching as the cops
follow him out.
I'm watching as the cops
follow him out.
Everyone's watching as the cops
follow him out.
She shakes her head, I smile
and bag my own stuff.
Change in hand,
I stop and buy a lottery ticket
on my way out.

Pittsburgh Love

Fires from the Monongahela
mills blister bright.
All knuckles and knotted
backs—like this, in our urban
bedroom we sweat,
choking on the phlegm
of our grandfathers
and the slack ink
of our own
pedestrian ways.

They were ugly
and meaty; we are careless
and mean, the way we
go down spitting
and begging—a false
fight for the scar
that lies molten
on the skin, the piece
of bone worked through
from the inside.

House Sitting

My mother took a cruise to Istanbul,
leaving me with the cats and a key
that won't work. Before she comes
back, I will change the locks and kill
at least one plant. I will begin
building the wall that says
"this side is me, this side is you."

I give her poems instead of children,
hangovers and no husband to assume
the watch she keeps. I won't commit
suicide, I promise, or move to California.
Instead, I buy a house three blocks away,
work nine to five, making nearly as much
as my sister who has two kids to raise.
Where does all the money go?

Before she comes back,
I will buy flowers for her birthday,
a spade for Mother's Day,
and plant the crocus bed
at the bottom of her stairs.
I will leave a note on the butcher's block
to say how much I missed her,
hoping she ate nice grapes
and met a man who spoke just enough
English to understand her.

And when she returns she will
stand outside the door staring
at the new metal knob, jiggling
the lock, call me from the neighbor's
with her baggage at her feet
to ask why, why she can't get in.

A Stormy Goodbye

Weather destroys such things
or makes them more beautiful.
Eyes in the squall brighter
than the whole of Saturn
ringed in light, they break
your heart for a moment
and then give it back.

Into the gale we look up
and dive down into our china
selves, sediments of graceful
last words said to dying mothers
and lovers lay crisp in the empty cup.
And we dare not wash it for fear
of surrendering the exquisite,
the residue of pain that keeps us rich,
keeps us thirsty, nearly whole.

Gravel

for Karen Demmler

I walk mincingly
from the carport
to the porch,
skin coarse with salt
and other sediment
I carry with me,
the August night
ripe with warm
tomatoes.

Single, I tread,
my arms full,
resting one bag
on my knee,
steadying the other
in the crook
of my elbow.
Peaches and corn
shift and buckle
as I search
for my keys,
like this,
never thinking
to put the bags
down or to make
another trip.

On Saturday
I meet friends
for coffee. Our life
is still a slumber party

in many ways—
telling secrets
of misguided love
and equally misguided
fingers and tongues;
laughing till we are weak
with struggling to be good,
till we cry because we
might never be good.
Still, we are comfortable
to be women, to be smart;
the edge of our catastrophes
we use to feed each other hope,
to dance.

Who else, I wonder,
could know all this,
place a finger on the heart
without flinching
from the very beat
of the thing?

Walking on Eggshells

She is cooking apologies
again, bringing him eggs
the way he likes them,
sunny-side up.

Watching the whites spit
in the pan, the yolks glisten
in their yellow mounds,
she prays he won't stir
before the coffee perks,
the toaster pops,
before she brushes her teeth,
combs the panic
from her hair.

But today is garbage day
and the gaping truck chews
trash beneath the window
as the dog in apartment one
cries to be let out.
And soon he will wake
to the hum of a hangover,
claws scraping at the door,
the noise of things thrown out.

That Close to Home

for Sam Maxwell II

Between breaths you fell
on that dingy strip of Penn Avenue,
the unexpected wrench of your heart
breaking your stride in front
of The Evergreen Tavern, the neon
"Stop and Go" swimming in the sky
as you hit the pavement, just short
of one mile—that close to home.

Somebody saw it—
the graceful Black man
collapsing in a pool of gray
sweats, the stopwatch clutched
in his palm—no ID, nothing
but an extra set of laces
and bus change. Someone called
911, kept you alive long enough
to get to the emergency room
where you lay in a coma
just six blocks from home
where dinner was waiting
and panic just beginning to set in.

I hope you heard singing
as they strapped you to the gurney,
Barry White and Isaac Hayes
circling your body as they did mine
the nights you worked over a sketch
in the sun room while I lay in bed
listening to the scratch of the needle,
the colors seeping up

through the floorboards—
painting me pretty, painting me safe.
How the different colors of our skin
paled in the shadow of that clean
hospital bed; rigged up with tubes
and monitors, your eyes burning
with what you gave, what was taken.

After three weeks Mom told them
to pull the plug, brought you home
where you lay in your graying skin,
bones pushing through the thin cover
of flesh until your body gave up,
the room silenced with what no longer
was and the woman who loved you
stroked your face as I watched:
one last time, like this, the fingertips
touching, trailing, letting go.

II.

Never to lie is to have no lock on your door.

— Elizabeth Baven

Behind the Irises

for Victor Curti

Vic calls me "diva,"
my eyeliner dark and thick,
the long black skirt
slit deliciously along
the curve of my thighs,
"Svelte," he says,
"damaging."
I light a smoke.

"You're simply radiant,"
he cries out, kissing me full
on the lips as we saunter
into the party room
and pour two glasses
of vodka with Roses,
positioning ourselves
in the candlelight
so flattering to the virile.

"Balsamic vinaigrette
is the key to the artichokes,"
he says, "and try the roasted
garlic with brie—to die
for"—I go to the bathroom
and look at myself bathed
in feigned ennui as I draw
a thin layer of Scarlet
Splendor across my lips.

We talk about "Charley,"
his pet name for men

who are hot and ready,
"He looks just like my friend,
Charley" or "Charley looks lonely,"
we whisper to one another,
seldom agreeing
on who Charley is:
I like them thin and dark,
he likes them muscular
and blonde—we'll never
fight over the same man.

He has other code names
like "Canadian" for men
who are gay. I say,
"Is he Canadian?" I don't know.
And Vic says, "A regular maple leaf."
"Ever done him?" I ask.
And he says he's careful
now and in love.

And I'm hopelessly
in love with this dreamy
man, taken with his penchant
for armoires and azaleas,
his flirting so brazen
and his quick, rich smile—
the thick dark sheen
of his hair inviting fingers
and the thin silver
of his smooth belt buckle.

I ask him about his friend
who tested positive
five years ago.
Pete's going to become
a trucker now, a big rig

guy driving loads of fresh
oranges and bananas
across the United States.
He's going to travel,
see everything he's missed.

"There's going to come a time,"
Vic says, fingers resting lightly
on his cuff, "The year of funerals,
when they'll all go down...
And I only own
one sports jacket."

"We can shop," I say
as he nods, pulling
a piece of lint
from his sleeve,
looking at me
from behind
a vase of white irises
just now
approaching
full bloom.

Make Me a Martini

and set it here
on the magazine table
where the glossy covers
wipe clean from the sweat.

Draw the bed sheets
back. Skin cool
in the dusk
and blue light of TV,
ice and olives
melt in our mouths,
leaving no space
for explaining
the things we do
to one another
at night.

Place your hand here
and let the dim draw
of morning hold
you where it hurts.
Like I could forget.
Like I could leave.
Like I could figure
on this day
being the last.

Eros and Thanatos on a Friday Night

for Danny Morrow

The next day, like a dream unreciprocated,
she remembered the angle of his bones
in the light of the brick cafe, flattering
as a visit from God: I will die with you
in this land of intellect and taxi drivers, she said.
But first we must shake loose the mysterious
and send pieces of it showering
over you, fairy dust settling like a cool
breath on the cusp of October.

She would, in fact, have died for wisdom
and the taxi driver weeping, but first
she must kiss him with the tongue of a sailor,
draw him near enough to smell the soap
on her shoulder. Infatuated, merciless,
holding ice to her wounds initially,
and then heat to do the healing.

White Noise

In the thick of August crab grass nights,
I thought about what I could have done
better, how I could make it good
the way my mother said it was
if you knew how to please a man.

Instead it had been a blunt break
and some blood; Jimmy's
mouth on mine, wet with spit
and cigarettes, and his useless
lumbering tongue. He said
he didn't know I was a virgin.
I said it didn't matter.
Still, I thought it would feel different,
wondered why I had said yes.

I guess I thought he would want me,
that he would stop being stupid
and poor, that he would call me
his girlfriend and hold my hand.
I liked the way his hair
fell across his slow boy face,
the way he came around late
after beers. I didn't know then
that he was drunk, that I too,
would come to need
some kind of buffer.

That thick room where he lived
with his mother—paint peeling,
water dripping, white noise—
endures in this blue longing,
and I am reminded of the sun

when I left that house,
pulled down by the weight
of the coming dark—
how I walked home late
on a school night pretending
I had found love, when what I found
was another job—the moon
the color of frosted whores
beating down, disappointed
in its own slow rise.

What It Might Look Like

I've lost my passport
just when another country
seems to be the only place
I could be without you.
I've spent nights looking
in old overnight bags
and drawers thick
with matches and paper clips,
finding an old post-it note
with "will you marry me?"
scrawled in red ink. I'm glad
I didn't. Red ink is bad luck.

Still, it's nice to know
someone once asked,
and I'm struck
by the longing I feel
with that note in my hand,
what it might look like
if you had written it,
how it flutters and almost
misses the trash.

The Wrap

He carries scotch tape in one pocket, plastic wrap
in another, wadded in a crinkled ball.
Each morning he fastens a new piece around
the cardboard sign to protect it from rain.

He works the early shift beneath the awning
of Schwartz's where I buy bagels each Friday,
and a large cup of coffee. Quarter to eight
and the weather is shitty again. Damp. Bone cold.

From another pocket he pulls a cigarette,
bent but not broken, and asks for a light.
I put down my bags of broccoli and pears,
fumble for a match and strike it.

"Them's is nice boots," he says, "Sharp,"
as I lean to keep the wind from extinguishing
the flame, cup my hand just inches from
his face, wishing I had worn my old kicks.

Crouching now, I'm face to face with his sign,
printed in black on corrugated cardboard:
"Please help. Homeless Vet. God Bless You."
It says again, like I have never read it before,

never heard it in my head with his voice.
Like a tombstone it leans against his leg,
the tails of his shirt drifting above the sidewalk,
the milk crate he sits on a dirty orange.

He thanks me for the light and I go to buy bagels—
raisin with cream cheese, juice and a large coffee,
knowing I should have asked what he likes.
Still, he smiles when I hand him the bag,

says he hasn't had breakfast and loves fresh juice.
I give him too much sugar, creamer and sweetener.
"I take it black," he says, and thanks me again
when I give him a dollar and a couple extra smokes.

"God bless you," he says as I turn to go.
And I tell him to take care, stay dry, to eat,
thinking how winter is just beginning,
how tomorrow I will ask him his name.

Skin Like a Blanket

The phone hasn't rung for three days
and just the thought of the treble
makes me tremble and pour another drink.
This is how loneliness is. You sink
inside it. Open the windows, shut
off the lights—breezes and shadows
lurking like a lover gone on a trip,
so far away you must pay in many ways
to call, so you sit idle with the cat
and a cigarette before the blue loom
of the TV. Did he mean it when he said
your poems were like tattoos,
your skin like a blanket, your cunt
like a cannonball ready to burst
as he shut the door behind him
leaving only the smell of gun powder
gone wet with the rain. The last trace
of his body long washed away,
the soap, a white sliver that slips
between your fingers leaving you
naked in the tub tracing your breast
with a finger, your nipples stiff
and cold, rising hard above the water,
the beat of your heart.

How to Change a Flat

The weather left me raw—
freezing sleet and leaning
wind icing my enthusiasm
for waving someone down.
Someone with a CB or a cell
phone, a jack and solid
workboots; someone
with a hard on to do
something good,
to get on his knees
and apply his weight
till the lug nuts give
and let go the grip.

I could've faced the storm,
the winter bearing down
like an avalanche of wet
mean dreams; stood out there
with my arms spread wide,
my head bowed against the gusts,
or at least I could've read
the manual, found a flare,
jammed a white rag
in the door. But I'm thinking
it's got to let up soon and what's
the worst that can happen?

It's only 7:00 and I can catch
the news; I can flash my lights
from inside where it's warm,
where just now a shameless
version of Sweet Jane begins
to play, my hand drifting in response—

the slight resistance of the tangled
skirt peeled beneath my coat,
the heel of my palm pressed
flat against my stomach, the first
touch of fingers brushing bare thighs
warm and wet under the frosted
highway lights. And I have half a tank
of gas—enough to write a letter,
enough to imagine telling you
about sex alone in the front seat,
headlights passing smoothly
across the windshield, the frigid
breath of January melting
from the inside out. How
when the flurry's spent,
mechanics mean so little
and the drive
is only the half of it.

Twenty-four Hours in Peoria, Illinois, 1984

In the soft hotel bed
I count breaths,
touch my stomach;
sleep is mean
and unreflective.

In the morning
you hold me, press
my palms like I am
strong enough for this,
stop short of thanking me,
and count the cash
in your wallet.

In a small room I wait
with girls who share
stories like candy:
how they'd die
if their parents
found out,
how they cried
when their parents
found out.
And I wonder if you
go to lunch:
what you would eat?

It is late when they
call my name
and I am thinking
I have to do this
so we can be

the way we were,
unchanged;
the way we are,
unchanged.

I lie on my back,
the nurse gently
spreading my legs.
"Breathe easy," she says,
"this is not the time for tears,"
but it is, I want to tell her,
it is a time for tears.

Paralysis

Susan Laviana was eleven,
maybe twelve, her tall, lanky
body ripe to be a model,
lying on the bed—pink canopy
and white posts—as her father
started the car in the garage.
She was killed by a hose taped
to the tailpipe while her mother
was out shopping for school clothes.

A call in October said Daddy had died
in a Florida hospital. If I had known,
maybe I would have been there. Then,
drinking vodka at Humphry's Good-Time
Saloon, I wanted to tell a stranger,
to get a date. But I told no one.
Went home. Missed my final exams.

Molly took pills in her dorm room
the night of the Beaux Arts Ball.
"An accidental mix of champagne
and sleeping pills," said her Catholic
family; not a suicide at all.
The tracheotomy, bloody
and unsuccessful, the pills lodged
in her stomach and veins.
And the scar on her throat
like the itch of wool as I bundle
up for another cold spell.

Winter and I am paralyzed,
unable to move this half of myself—
the half that carried hope like a stone,

knowing my mother made the right choice,
bringing her lover—my stepfather—
home to die in the dining room
where we ate. His body wasted
and bony on the couch.
She, bending over him,
scraping mucus from his mouth
and me, walking to the door,
leaving before the body was removed.

The Jealous Poem

I could tell everyone
that you ruined
the party when
with the third Tanqueray,
reminiscences
turned to riot.

Running
out of ice cubes:
it's a nightmare,
and everybody's
left with their hands
in their pockets
and their cheeks
sucked dry
from the inside.

I could wring my hands
on a public bench,
"What's wrong," they
would say, complete strangers
wanting to know
about the dream
where you sleep with her,
one breast like another
and she strokes you
with nimble fingers
so you think
you have escaped.

Wrapping yourself around
her small frame, you can feel
the yellow of her bones;

find the "righteous" in her
cool-child hips urging you
past the hollow breath
of morning when you might
begin again
to think of flesh.

1965

for my mother, Jeanne Scardamalia

One lay inside her womb,
two others already clinging
to her leg and breast.
Relentless, I imagine,
this kicking and bumping
from inside and out.

And without a silk dress
or a willing husband
to slide it from
her shoulders
in the hour
before plates
begin their clattering
and fingers reach
out to be filled.

The feeding, the petting,
the fixing, the patting,
until one morning,
she can't any more.

Let her husband sleep
far from her
in another room,
in another state
altogether, in a
weaker woman's arms.

Let the children eat
caramels and play

way past the hour
of street lights
leaving their pink coats
neglected on the stairs,
running like
some crazy
cartoon animals
in the dusk.
And she will lay
her head down
on this pillow,
hung to dry
in the August sun;
the tears in her eyes,
lightning in the sky
threatening
the kind of promise
that drenches.

Bar Tour: A Cheap Retrospect

Past this, you say,
is where we met
wet and hungry,
lean and smoking
cigarettes—no reason
for going home.

Past this, you think,
is where we
broke small things,
spoke in syllables
and rattled
change
in our pockets.

Past this, you know,
is where we opened
the door—the night
winds whipping in—
and one of us
drifted right out.
One of us
went
right out.

I Call You Friday Afternoon
and You Answer

My sister's voice rings lucent
on the other end, expecting
a call from a system user
or her husband who will bring
home milk. She is writing
source codes, heating formula;
her hands flash across
the keyboard, the phone
cinched between
her shoulder and chin.
The click of keys stops
and she asks, "What's wrong?"

I tell her I need to know
what she thinks of our father,
did she ever visit the grave?
What does she remember
about the funeral, could it
have been so hot in October?
Why can't I recall laying
a flower or something
on the casket? Remembering
the hole in the dresser
where his fist hit cheap wood,
his hand on my thigh, moist
and too scared to move,
I ask if he ever touched her.

"Are you saying
he *touched* you?" she says.
I wasn't.
"He never hit us," she says.

I know.
"He was just a lousy father
in the end...selfish."
*He left everything
to his second wife.*

I can hear that she is typing
again: the clack of the key
board is the rhythm
of a small train
pushing through.

"I miss him too,"
she says, "when I see
my Karl raise his small
fist and strike out
at his sister,
when I see her
turn away."

A Drink with Daddy

Why bother to be genuine
about love when the world
is so very lopsided, silly.
Like searching for your father
in a bar 10 years later
(awkward and embarrassing
to carry *that* around).
She'd leave it outside
in social situations,
but here it was before her,
the ageless longing
settling quietly
in the bottom
of a highball.

Careful Crossing

for my grandmother, Bianca Contrucci

For the first time she says, "It's not fair,"
and I want to put a red scarf
around her hair, slip whiskey in her tea,
stir it with honey and white milk.

God could have been more imaginative
than this, or less—the way Grandma
can't finish a page or her lunch
of canned peaches and broth;
how she has to ask to be cleaned—
wiped clean—when so much
has already been scrubbed
from her paper skin.

Sunlight makes me run for cover.
I fight the urge to shut the shades
and leave the room when she says,
"You are such a beautiful young
girl. Can't you see?"

I try hard to tell her how much I hate
what I am living and not living,
light a cigarette in that sacred
room. And all the while she smiles,
nodding at my abandoned face,
watching me smoke.

In the dust of the brocade light
I take her hand from beneath
the bleached throw and squeeze
as if to break her from this mindful

gratitude; her eyes strong and steady,
ever patient, ever ready,
hope forever cradled
in the palm of my hand.

Making it Right

This morning your mother died
and all we could talk about
was flowers—day lilies, lilacs,
paper whites—growing
wild in a yard once ripe
with berries. Your lean face
pressed against the phone
calling some order
to the tangle, the hush
and loss of the woman
who put coffee grinds
beneath the rose bush,
pulled weeds from
the thick ground cover.

All the tending to rows,
a need to put things right;
but there's no right
to moving the body
through the house to the garage
where an open hearse waits,
and no right to the stupid setting
of teacups on the mantle.
And all I want to do is call you back,
love you blind out of this still August air.

But I leave because you ask me to
and drive back to the place
where the lawn needs mowing
and the basil has gone to seed.
Where we fill the hole
with growing things—
not so neat and planned,

but no less rooted in beauty—
where I arrange cut flowers
in a vase—daisies and mums,
warm water and aspirin—
nurturing what's left
of our own mad longing.

III.

In my mind, abandonment may be worse than abuse.
Most kids live through abuse, but if you just put them in a trash
can, they die.

— Sapphire

Big Tongue

Everything was big about the night,
the backdrop of the city sprawling
lazy, its three-river arms and bracelet
bridges beneath the big wet sky.
Big drinks filling big voids
around the bar—tumblers full
of the unrequited. The British
soccer boys lining the deck
looking beyond the city of steel
to the next round of Bass
and Budweisers. And your body,
as solid as the girders that buoy
the bridges in their relentless
coming and going, hovering
close, scraping the midnight stars
as I toyed brilliant in small
desires and leather.

Simple really, the immediate
press of bone to bone balanced
over the hood of the car.
You with leverage, me licentious
beneath the banner of banter
that paced this curious coupling.
I could have fucked you right then,
but you said in a breath
of bewilderment, in the guise
of frank civility, that I had a big tongue,
the very shock of the discovery
blocking the next opening,
forcing me to light a cigarette
in the midst of my abandon
and consider my freakish nature.

Just imagine a big man like you
gagging on my small-girl tongue.
It would make the news, make
the *Guinness Book of World Records*,
make the morning a bit more difficult
to rationalize; me having swallowed
hard all these years without choking.

Resisting the Fall

1972 and the Hill, far from my
Greentree home though just
the other side of the Fort Pitt Tunnels,
was a place where Black
people lived—people like Sam—
and he went there each night
in our beige Volkswagen,
returned late and crawled
into bed by my mother.

And that night we picked
him up: me wide awake
to the new night and mom,
eager too, the way she was
each time he walked towards the car,
his body filling the small air
with Old Spice, his hand
on her thigh as she drove.

I remember waiting
and waiting, finding
my way to the clinic wall
and the cement ramp below,
lost in the bustle and lights
of the paramedics, the shaking
of heads and shuffling of feet.

Seven years old and waiting for Sam.

I stood mesmerized by the crumpled man,
his skull like a squashed pea;
the bottle of Mad Dog smashed,
and the thin brown liquid seeping

into the cracks of his skin
before my mother urged me away,
her eyes mirroring fright, wishing
she had left me tucked safely
in bed where the only blood
that ran was through my
small-fisted heart,
and pain never crashed
in a heap on the sidewalk,
but balanced carefully,
resisting the fall for years.

The Shrinking of Pittsburgh

I'm waiting for the day
I don't love you anymore
and I suspect it will come
quietly, the way we
stopped calling
and just looked away.

I've seen you walk
up the wrong side
of the street and I've
walked down the other,
showing my indifference,
hoping you'd notice.

I've heard people say
that Pittsburgh is a really
small town. It's getting smaller,
I swear, each time we pass.

Ten Copies and A Condom

Walk in and order ten copies
of a poem. Watch the clerk
feed dimes into the dirty Canon
beast, slamming the lid
with each cock-eyed duplicate
until she spies the word "suck."
What? You never did it?
Never took a cock in your mouth
like candy, like a snack?

"We don't carry condoms,"
she says in reply to your request.
"We're a family store."
And you think about the boy
in slick hair and leather,
ready to take what's offered
for the holy bliss of a tongue:
sweet satisfaction, validation,

cum on down to Co-Gos,
where given the chance
they could stop at nothing:
gasoline, garters, dairy, dildos,
big gulps and butt plugs.
An endless supply of gum and mints
for close-ups and tongue-fucks,
licking and kissing. Sex
and convenience, genius
on a corner; a one-stop-shop
for two pet boys looking for a good

time to be careful,
raincoats and gloves—

don't get any on you.
Gas, I don't need no gas,
Whatchu want with a poem, baby
when you can have me?
Don't know.
Ten copies.
No condom.

Prayin' Cheap

Landing dinner on the company card Friday
night, the drinks roll over like so many waitresses
on a stiff shift at the Clark Bar. Buy a round for the friends
of a client—real square boys with shares in General Electric,
safe corners with streetlights; they all curb their dogs.

"What do you do?" I say to the lawyer and pocket a chip
good for another somewhere down the road, sometime
when I'm runnin' light on wit and circumstances beyond
my wallet got me layin' low. He doesn't notice the half of it—
the two-bit smile I give him when he mentions my tattoo,
the bend of my ass when I reach for a match.

I got friends here that aren't scared of quittin',
Aren't scared of gettin' in up to their elbows. We know
that whether you're shovelin' it in or shovelin' it out,
it's all dirt. And that ain't so bad, comin' home wicked
on gin and Jesus men who pray you keep up the sweat,
pray your loyalty is like a mirror, lookin' at themselves
for the first time, wishin' they knew how to dance like that.

After the Sled Ride

In the basement the dryer whirled
with wet snowsuits, socks
and sweaters soiled at the cuffs
as we marched around in thin
undershirts, our chests just finding
the press of a nipple beneath,
the warmth of the dryer, moist
on pink legs and cotton panties.

I was a leader. Careless
in my naked costume, parading
like a Queen drawn to adoration.
Barbie ever summered in her camper,
Ken ever ready to rescue her
from the mountainous wet boots,
the avalanche of unlucky weather
awaiting her as she drove blindly
into the rubber Adirondacks.
And the bears, anxious for a taste
of her smooth symmetrical thighs.

There were no boys back then,
only blind little animals in their
Tough-Skin jeans, scabby and stupid
with riotous words and flushed faces
still outside on their toboggans
scaling Killer Hill, roaring down
like warriors until dusk
when the streetlights came on.
Then their mothers called loudly
with promises and threats
and like thieves, resentful
of the coming dark, they hid
behind bushes, throwing snowballs

all the way up Kelly Alley
till their cheeks stung and someone
landed facedown in the berm.

They didn't know how to play yet,
those boys, how to save Barbie
from the falling, how to carry her
in their strong Ken arms away
from the ravages of the bear,
all growls and teeth, how to heal
her perilous broken legs with a gift
of penny candy and a new sequined
outfit. Only we could script
this kind of joy. Only we knew
we were playing for keeps.

Certain Bonds

"It was hell," my mother says,
"walking down the aisles
of the grocery pregnant, knowing
I would never make his lunch again."

My father left then came back
all surprises and candy,
with a twenty-five dollar bond
and a new crib. Wet blue eyes
that fired black at the breaking
of a dish, the dog that wouldn't
come, the wife who wouldn't
stop asking for love.

My brother says he threw things.
My mother, that he smacked
our heads as he passed the table.
My sister says he punched holes
in the wall, and he did.

Still, the memory I have
is that twenty-five dollar bond.
And this picture. This picture
of my father inscribed on the back:
*be kind, be gentle
and never hurt intentionally.*

In it, he is sitting on the rim
of a Philadelphia fountain
wearing a purple shirt
with laced cords at the neck,
a denim jacket, faded jeans,
and a face that says with certainty
a bullet can change everything.

Different Colored Shoes

are OK in the dark;
on the wrong feet,
OK, but they hurt.
And for losers like us,
any amount of vodka
is good. And sex
is a perk; jerkin' off,
a talent, and writing
drunk the only way
to say some thing
that counts.

For what it's worth,
I've only had one
and already,
my socks feel
like cocoons—
smaller than sin
on a rainy day.

Darlington Road

Today the sky is broken,
the sun slicing through
at odd angles. Clouds
jarred by scars of light,
and winter scattered
everywhere. Scuffling
with a list of errands,
I shift bags, clumsy
in the snow, unbuttoned
and uncertain of where
to go next.

The line at the post
office shuffles
with the damp
press of bodies
in fat boots, nickels
stumbling over gloved
fingers like hardtack.
And asking for a receipt
is senseless—stamps
already stuck
in the moist breath
of exchange
that grows with each
opening and closing
of the door, and dusk
crawling in at four
from behind
heavy windows.

I slide the wrinkled
envelope in the slot

marked "local"
and slip out into
the chill and thickening
night, headlights
glinting off fragments
of ice and salt.
I picture myself stooping
to pick up the pieces
and letting them
fall on Darlington,
where the homes,
tucked in drifts
that cover stairs
and walks, blush
in their yellow lamp-lit
beds—shoveled
out, plowed in,
unmistakably owned.

Navigating

My life has not unfolded
like a paper plane,
all angles and purpose,
but like a child's toy
that opens and shuts
exposing thin dreams
with the lift of a flap,
each careless choice
determining the next.

Tonight at The Cage
with the whole of it
stretched flat across the bar,
I press out the creases
and draw a map to navigate
the next fifty years,
plotting the next random
guess and its answer.
Getting things down on paper,
making a plan, ordering
another gin and tonic.

I stop here nearly
every night
and they know me.
I'm the one who folds
swans and bow ties
out of dollar bills,
leaves them as tips
for the barmaid
who is sweet
and untethered,
the color of wind

on her cheeks
and the bristling
of purpose in her
walk; flying here
and there with orders—
two Jim Beams
and a draft—
counting change.

And at the end
of the night, the smell
of chlorine and comet
on her hands, she pours
herself a stiff one
and sums it all up—
like everyone,
straightening the bills
to spend with the rest.

The Body that Dances for You

I call off work the night before
and wake late. Already
I am thinking about what I've done—
the cookies, the crackers, the bread
and chocolate, batter hardening
on the counter. I am counting
the sit-ups I will do to fit into
the jeans that sling low on the hips,
draw looks from boys in bars;
the body that dances for you
in heels and garters.

Five pounds here, another drink,
way too many cigarettes.
Always filling, always feeling
short of full—the distended
belly of a child. I brush my teeth,
drink coffee, wait for the laxative
to work. Brush crumbs
from the sheets, from my hair,
gather wrappers left crumpled
on the night stand

and think of my father,
the dream where he is thin
and brittle with diabetes, curled
on the floor, his legs useless,
face bloated, eyes begging forgiveness
for ice cream and Salems;
open sores that never healed,
half-empty prescription bottles
rattling in the cabinet
long after the funeral.

Then alone in the comfort
of empty cupboards and chores,
I test my sugar and take insulin—
the garbage sealed and dragged
to the trash, the dishwasher
churning, the smell of Lysol
as I mop the bathroom floor,
clean vomit from the toilet.

Sins

for my sister, Wendy Mallorey

In the family room
I watch her sleep,
the children put down
for the night; her
husband in his shop
filling baby food jars
with nails and screws.

*

In her dream
  Wendy is dancing
  and she is thin,
  running her fingers
  over bones, counting
  each rib like the rings
  of a tree. Fossils,
  they appear
  after years of erosion
  and she gloats,
  refusing dessert,
  already full
of her own flesh
hauled heavy
into the reclining chair
night after night.
The blue TV light
glowing faint around
her marriage, the very
weight of it scooped
into a second bowl
of ice cream.

*

I sit beside her with fruit,
my finger scarred
from years of purging—
full then empty
full then empty—
watching her body
heave with passion,
something sweet.

*

She wakes restless,
asks if I've seen
her recipe for scalloped
potatoes—the one
that went over
like gangbusters
at the last block party.

Leafing through cards
in the rolodex she keeps next
to the sofa, fingers laced
between "twice-baked"
and "lyonnaise" she wonders
how I stay so thin.
It's easier, I say, *when
you don't have children.
Go back to sleep.*

I draw the comforter up
around her chest,
tuck in the edges;
my own body

covering hers,
the sins you can see,
the sins you can't.

Love Isn't Enough

for Sue Clifton

All around the city the girls are starving
and boys nap through dinner in bar
room booths. The clatter of platters echoes
as mothers serve heartache and the dog
gnaws her paw in the pantry.

In back, the fathers mount up, saddled
and sandwiched with bits of dried meat
in their pockets. Parched to the spleen
they fill their canteens with just enough juice
to keep their lips moist and hearts dry

on the hard ride to the home of the mistress
and her bony children waiting for beef jerky
and a taste of family life. "It's all gone spoiled,"
the woman says to her therapist on the verge
of a breakthrough. "And I'm hungry all of the time."

Rare Space

"Where did you learn that?"
you ask, and I can't remember
learning anything—
walking, talking, spitting—

Your cock in my mouth
is water in a glass
and like a long-distance runner
I drink deep at the seventh mile,
the quench filling
the space
between the mouth
and the heart.

It's Not the Heat, It's the Humidity

The city is a swamp tonight,
a sponge soaking light
from the dank sky, breeding
malcontent like malaria
as the crickets beat
their wet wings in song.
The bodies of the young
slog together in pools
of liquid languor,
streetlights bent
with the very weight
of sin grown heavy
in the heat.

We suffer the sweat,
damp fans inching their blades
in a circle, cutting through
the curdled air that sends us
weary to the frigidaire
for another cube of ice.
Ripe to endure the city's
mean tar, neon singeing
the night like a gypsy scarf,
our minds swelter, edge us closer
to the window in the tepid
midnight to touch our moist
breasts and pray for the sun
to break its cruel hover;
let us wash clean the soiled
sheets, the yellowed shirts,
and touch with grace again
our own willing skin.

I Might

for Thomas J. McIlroy

I'm finding pieces of you,
as if the day I turned thirty
marked the march back,
the long walk back
to collect the things I want—
the coffee cup, the toy
train, the thin pajamas
bleached and dried
to a weight that barely covers
the bark of my skin—
the Polaroid of the small
man, his narrow fist
and sunken shoulders
lost among scraps
I keep locked in a green
metal box.

My lover is forty-six,
the same age as you
when you finally faltered
in your Florida home,
swelling with diabetes
like a sponge; a shell-skinny
man in a hospital bed
with another wife,
another life altogether.
One bad pill
and your heart failed,
it failed and you died,
leaving before anyone
told you that I might

love you again some day,
that I might not.

Goodbye Valentine

I have begged the angels
to appear, calling
out through fevered
skies, sins revisited
and halos half-cocked—
I can hear them whispering
that this is only practice.

I have asked them
to come on Sundays
when loneliness
takes its bath,
emerging clean
and vital. Naked,
a little girl, she drips
and picks the scab
from her knee;
like last week
and next week
it bleeds again.

Today Michelangelo
says a prayer,
alone on the scaffolding
high in the air:
when the angels rise—
flushed cheeks
and open jackets—
that he might put away
his red paint
having finished the heart.

Big Brain

This extra twenty pounds
is my brain getting bigger
everyday—things you can't know
in your small-boned frame. Slim
is not a word you would use
to describe me, though I can fake
waif on call, like a doll
with three answers for everything:
"Yes," "I will," and "It's my fault."

I take off my shirt and you say
my breasts are much larger
than you imagined. Just imagine
if you could open my skull,
what a heap would fall
in your lap and anchor you
there till I was done talking.
Boulders of rebel thought
weighing you down, an avalanche
of fantastic reason that could
bury you alive.

Truth is not this heavy,
but the seeking of truth
is like a grand piano on the back
of a stooge, wavering, balancing,
moving forward with pain
and awkward gestures
in a comedy of elephants.
Even I am laughing as I stumble,
my neck quivering beneath
the ever-growing load
of day-old wisdom.

And therein lies the beauty
of this big brain o' mine.
No hat can contain it,
no beast can tame it.
It is fat with acceptance,
bulging with desire,
refusing narrow spaces,
the walls of skin and bone.

Debts

Wrestling with silence
that stretches far
into the afternoon,
our mouths lie open
only to the bite of vodka,
the arched likeness
of old lovers. We bite back,
lips bruised with the dismissal
of hope and the fear
that something
tangible will claim us.

Fallen to the carpet,
brush burns hot and red
from scraping close,
we cannot care about tomorrow,
we cannot talk about the past.
The lessons breathe back
through our lungs
like hot milk scalding
our throats. We flinch
and set fire to everything
that needs burning.

Biography

Leslie Anne Mcilroy is an advertising copywriter for The Kaiser Group. She is also Managing Editor/cofounder of HEArt —Human Equity Through Art—a Pittsburgh-based non-profit group publishing the nation's only journal of literature and art devoted to confronting discrimination and promoting social justice. Her awards include the Slipstream Poetry Chapbook Competition prize for her chapbook *Gravel* and first place in the 1997 Chicago Literary Awards Competition, judged by Gerald Stern. Her poems have been published in numerous journals and anthologies including *American Poetry: The Next Generation*, the *Emily Dickinson Award Anthology*, the *Eclectic Literary Forum*, *Henry's Creature: Poems and Stories on the Automobile*, *The Ledge*, *Main Street Rag*, *The MacGuffin*, *The Mississippi Review*, *The Pittsburgh City Paper*, *The Pittsburgh Post-Gazette* and *The Pittsburgh Quarterly*. She lives in Pittsburgh, Pennsylvania with her punky dog Zelda, the infamous Butt-Cat, and her shameless friend and lover Galen.